CRYPTO'S CARE

BLOCKCHAIN'S BATTLE WITH THE ENVIRONMENT

Ryan Carrington

Crypto's Carbon Conundrum:
Blockchain's Battle with the Environment
Part of the Crypto Crash Course Series

Copyright © 2024 RJ Carrington
All rights reserved.

The author asserts the moral right to be identified as the creator of this work. No part of this publication may be reproduced, distributed, or transmitted in any form or by any means, including photocopying, recording, or other electronic or mechanical methods, without the prior written permission of the author, except in the case of brief quotations embodied in reviews or critical articles and certain other noncommercial uses permitted by copyright law. For permission requests, contact the author at ryancarrington@proton.me.

This book contains research from publicly available sources, and while every effort has been made to ensure the accuracy of the information presented, the author does not claim ownership of facts, data, or publicly available knowledge. All interpretations, conclusions, and commentary are the original work of the author.

ISBN: 9798342645157 / 9798343646702
First Edition: 2024
Published by Ryan Carrington

Disclaimer	4
Introduction: The Crypto-Carbon Conundrum	6
1. Blockchain's Environmental Impact: Uncovering the Hidden Costs	14
2. Real-World Consequences: How Blockchain is Shaping Our Planet	22
3. Greener Pastures: Sustainable Solutions for Blockchain	34
4. The Future of Blockchain's Environmental Impact	46
5. Taking Action: How You Can Engage with Eco-Friendly Blockchain Solutions	56
Conclusion: Blockchain's Green Future—What's Next?	66
Glossary of Terms	74
A Final Note from the Author	76
Books in This Series	78
Get Exclusive Previews!	82
About the Author	84

DISCLAIMER

The content in this book, **"Crypto's Carbon Conundrum: Blockchain's Battle with the Environment,"** is provided for informational and educational purposes only. It is not intended as financial, investment, legal, or professional advice. Every effort has been made to ensure the accuracy of the information presented, but the author and publisher make no guarantees regarding the completeness, reliability, or timeliness of the content. Cryptocurrency markets, blockchain technology, and environmental concerns are rapidly evolving, and the reader is encouraged to perform their own research and seek professional guidance before making decisions related to these topics.

The tools, platforms, services, and technologies mentioned in this book are discussed for illustrative purposes and should not be interpreted as endorsements. The author and publisher do not endorse or recommend any specific services or platforms. Readers should evaluate all options independently based on their own needs and circumstances.

The author and publisher are not responsible for any actions taken based on the information provided in this book. Readers should be aware that investments in cryptocurrency and blockchain projects carry significant risk, and past performance is not indicative of future results. It is essential to conduct thorough research and consider your own risk tolerance before engaging in these activities.

Additionally, while environmental solutions and green initiatives are discussed in this book, the author and publisher do not guarantee the effectiveness of any specific practices, tools, or technologies mentioned. Readers are encouraged to stay informed about the latest developments in sustainability, blockchain technology, and environmental impact and adopt best practices accordingly.

By reading this book, you agree that the author and publisher are not liable for any losses, damages, or legal consequences that may arise from your use of the information contained herein.

INTRODUCTION: THE CRYPTO-CARBON CONUNDRUM

What's at Stake?

Blockchain technology has rapidly grown from a niche innovation to a global phenomenon, revolutionizing industries like finance, supply chain management, and even art. Cryptocurrencies, led by Bitcoin and Ethereum, have become household names, often hailed as the future of money and decentralization. But beneath the surface of these digital wonders lies a significant and often overlooked issue—the environmental cost that accompanies this technological leap forward.

At the heart of blockchain's environmental impact is its reliance on energy-intensive processes, particularly the **Proof of Work** (PoW) consensus mechanism, which powers major cryptocurrencies like Bitcoin. The process of mining, which involves solving complex mathematical problems to validate transactions, requires vast amounts of computational power. This isn't just a minor issue; the electricity consumption for Bitcoin mining alone is comparable to that of entire countries. As of recent estimates, Bitcoin's annual energy consumption rivals that of countries like Argentina and the Netherlands, placing blockchain technology at the center of global environmental debates.

Why is this such a pressing issue? In a world grappling with the effects of climate change, every industry and individual is under scrutiny for their carbon footprint. The very fact that blockchain is poised to revolutionize so many sectors makes it a potential ally in the fight against inefficiencies, but it also means it cannot escape the growing demand for sustainability. As the use of cryptocurrencies and blockchain applications grows, so too does the energy required to sustain them, which in turn leads to increased carbon emissions.

Critics argue that blockchain's environmental cost may be too high, especially in regions where the majority of mining operations are powered by non-renewable energy sources like coal. On the other hand, proponents of the technology highlight that it is still in its early stages, with ample room for improvement. Can blockchain evolve without becoming an ecological burden? Or will it become another industry that exacerbates global environmental challenges?

In this book, we'll delve into these pressing questions, exploring the fine line blockchain walks between innovation and environmental responsibility. We'll uncover both the undeniable challenges and the emerging opportunities that could make blockchain more sustainable. If we ignore the environmental consequences, blockchain could become one of the most significant obstacles to reducing global carbon emissions. However, there is also potential for blockchain to lead the way in green innovation, provided the right changes are made. With the right focus on sustainability, blockchain technology can evolve in ways that align with the broader goal of a cleaner, more sustainable future.

Blockchain's Promise vs. Reality

Blockchain is often hailed as a revolutionary force with the potential to disrupt industries and reshape economies. Its promise lies in its **decentralized** nature, which offers transparency, security, and efficiency without relying on traditional intermediaries like banks or governments. However, while the technology has garnered praise for its innovation, the **reality** of its energy consumption often gets overshadowed by the excitement surrounding its potential.

At the core of blockchain's promise is the idea of a decentralized future where people can transact, create, and collaborate without the need for centralized authorities. The **blockchain ledger**, which records every transaction, is maintained across multiple nodes around the world, providing unparalleled security. This system is particularly appealing for financial systems, supply chain transparency, and even **decentralized finance (DeFi)**, where users can engage in peer-to-peer financial activities without the intervention of traditional banking institutions.

However, this **utopian vision** comes with a hefty energy price tag. For cryptocurrencies like Bitcoin, maintaining this decentralized network relies on the **Proof of Work** (PoW) mechanism. This requires miners to solve cryptographic puzzles to validate transactions and add them to the blockchain. The more miners there are, the more difficult these puzzles become, leading to an ever-increasing demand for **computational power**. As more computers engage in this energy-intensive race, the network becomes more secure, but at the cost of consuming vast amounts of electricity.

The reality is that this consumption has created a dilemma. While blockchain has the potential to offer **efficiency** and **security**, it is currently contributing to a significant environmental burden. Studies have shown that the annual energy consumption of Bitcoin alone exceeds that of several nations, with estimates suggesting it consumes more electricity than entire countries like Norway or Switzerland. This has sparked debates about whether the benefits of blockchain outweigh its environmental cost. Can blockchain truly be the solution to inefficiencies if its environmental impact is so severe?

It's crucial to recognize that blockchain is still a young technology, and its energy consumption issues are not an inherent flaw but a challenge that innovators are working to address. Emerging alternatives like **Proof of Stake (PoS)** and **Layer 2 solutions** are already offering more sustainable options, but the **reality** is that blockchain's environmental footprint must be acknowledged and addressed before it can fully realize its potential as a transformative force.

In the chapters that follow, we'll explore how the blockchain community is grappling with this paradox—balancing its revolutionary potential with the urgent need to minimize its environmental impact. While blockchain's promise is undeniable, its **reality** is more complicated, and understanding this complexity is crucial to envisioning a future where blockchain can thrive without devastating the planet.

Myths vs. Facts

The rise of cryptocurrencies like Bitcoin has been accompanied by widespread concern over their environmental impact, with headlines often portraying blockchain as an unmitigated **energy guzzler**. While it's true that blockchain networks, particularly those using **Proof of Work (PoW)**, do consume significant amounts of energy, the picture is more nuanced than it may first appear. In this section, we'll dissect some of the most common **misconceptions** surrounding blockchain's carbon footprint and separate fact from fiction.

One of the most pervasive myths is that all **cryptocurrencies** are equally harmful to the environment. Bitcoin, being the first and most well-known cryptocurrency, is often the poster child for critiques of blockchain energy consumption. However, not all blockchains operate in the same way. Bitcoin relies on the **PoW** mechanism, which is indeed energy-intensive, but many newer blockchains are adopting **Proof of Stake (PoS)**, a far more energy-efficient alternative. In fact, Ethereum, the second-largest cryptocurrency, has made the transition to PoS, significantly reducing its energy use. This distinction is crucial when evaluating the environmental impact of blockchain as a whole.

Another misconception is that **Bitcoin mining** operations are entirely powered by non-renewable energy. While it's true that in certain regions, miners rely heavily on coal or other fossil fuels, the reality is more complex. A substantial portion of Bitcoin mining occurs in areas where renewable energy sources, such as **hydropower**, are abundant. For example, studies suggest that in some regions of China, where much of Bitcoin mining has historically taken place, a significant amount of the electricity used comes from **hydroelectric** power plants. Furthermore, miners are increasingly seeking out locations with cheap, excess renewable energy, driven by both economic incentives and growing environmental concerns.

It's also important to note that comparisons of **Bitcoin's energy consumption** to that of entire nations often overlook a key detail: **efficiency**. While Bitcoin's overall energy consumption is high, it also supports a **global financial network** that operates independently of traditional banking systems, which themselves consume significant amounts of energy. The environmental costs of printing money, powering financial institutions, and maintaining the physical infrastructure of traditional banks are rarely factored into these comparisons. When viewed through a broader lens, the energy consumption of blockchain networks like Bitcoin is still considerable but not as disproportionate as some critics suggest.

That said, the concerns over blockchain's energy use are not unfounded. As the demand for cryptocurrency continues to grow, so does the energy required to support these networks, particularly those relying on PoW. However, the notion that blockchain technology is irredeemably harmful to the environment is a misconception. **Innovation** in the space is rapidly evolving, with many projects actively seeking solutions to reduce their carbon footprint. Technologies like **Layer 2 solutions**, **sidechains**, and even blockchain's integration with carbon offset programs are already in play, aiming to mitigate these environmental challenges.

While blockchain certainly has an environmental impact, it's essential to distinguish between **fact and hyperbole**. Bitcoin and other cryptocurrencies are not as universally destructive as some suggest, and with the ongoing development of **sustainable blockchain**

solutions, the narrative around blockchain's carbon footprint is beginning to change. As we move forward in this book, we'll explore these solutions in detail, offering a clearer understanding of where blockchain truly stands in the **battle with the environment**.

A Journey of Solutions

While the environmental challenges posed by blockchain technology are significant, there is reason for optimism. The industry is not turning a blind eye to its carbon footprint, and in fact, many innovators are actively seeking ways to make blockchain more energy-efficient and environmentally friendly. This section will explore the cutting-edge solutions being developed to address the energy consumption issues associated with blockchain, providing a glimpse into how the technology might evolve in the future.

One of the most promising avenues for reducing blockchain's environmental impact is the shift away from **Proof of Work (PoW)** to more sustainable consensus mechanisms like **Proof of Stake (PoS)**. Unlike PoW, which requires miners to compete using vast amounts of computational power, PoS allows validators to secure the network based on the amount of cryptocurrency they hold and are willing to "stake" as collateral. This eliminates the need for energy-intensive mining while maintaining the same level of security and decentralization. **Ethereum**, one of the largest blockchain platforms, has already made this transition, demonstrating that large-scale networks can move towards more sustainable models without sacrificing functionality.

Beyond the transition to PoS, other innovative solutions are being developed to reduce the energy requirements of blockchain networks. **Layer 2 scaling solutions** are a prime example. These systems work by processing transactions off the main blockchain and only settling the final result on-chain. By moving the bulk of the computational work off the main network, Layer 2 solutions dramatically reduce the energy consumed for each transaction. Projects like the **Lightning Network** for Bitcoin and **Optimistic Rollups** for Ethereum are leading the way in this area, allowing for faster, cheaper, and more energy-efficient transactions.

Another exciting development is the rise of **carbon offset initiatives** within the blockchain space. Some projects are actively working to counterbalance their energy consumption by investing in carbon offset programs, funding renewable energy projects, or using their technology to promote environmental sustainability. **Chia**, a blockchain that uses a unique consensus mechanism called **Proof of Space and Time**, has positioned itself as a more environmentally friendly alternative to PoW-based blockchains. The Chia network consumes far less energy, and the project is also focused on offsetting any emissions it does generate.

Finally, there is a growing movement within the blockchain community to use this technology for **environmental good**. Blockchain's transparency and immutability make it an ideal tool for tracking carbon credits, monitoring supply chains for sustainability, and verifying the authenticity of eco-friendly claims. For example, platforms like **Power Ledger** are using blockchain to track and trade renewable energy, allowing consumers to buy and sell excess solar power with ease. These kinds of applications show that blockchain doesn't have to be part of the problem—it can also be part of the solution.

As we continue, these solutions will be explored in greater depth, showcasing the innovations that are already taking shape to ensure that blockchain can thrive without leaving a significant ecological footprint. The environmental future of blockchain depends not only on recognizing the problem but also on implementing these solutions at scale. The road ahead is filled with opportunities for the technology to become more sustainable, and the ongoing efforts to improve its environmental impact offer a hopeful glimpse into what's possible.

What To Expect In This Book

In this book, we will dive deep into the environmental challenges that blockchain technology faces, examining its current carbon footprint while exploring the innovative solutions being developed to address these issues. From the shift to more energy-efficient consensus mechanisms like **Proof of Stake** to the rise of **carbon offset initiatives** and **Layer 2 solutions**, we'll look at how the industry is evolving to become more sustainable. You'll also find real-world examples, case studies, and actionable steps that can help you engage with greener blockchain platforms. Let's dive in!

1. BLOCKCHAIN'S ENVIRONMENTAL IMPACT: UNCOVERING THE HIDDEN COSTS

1.1: The Energy-Hungry Machines: Proof of Work & Mining

At the core of blockchain's energy consumption is the **Proof of Work (PoW)** mechanism, the foundation of many early cryptocurrencies like Bitcoin. Designed to ensure the security and decentralization of the network, PoW works by requiring miners to solve complex mathematical puzzles to validate transactions. These puzzles are not easy—intentionally so—because the difficulty of the computation ensures that any attempt to alter or attack the network would require an enormous amount of computational power, making fraud virtually impossible.

However, this security comes at a cost. The process of mining requires specialized hardware, often called **ASICs (Application-Specific Integrated Circuits)**, which are designed solely for the purpose of mining. These machines run constantly, consuming vast amounts of electricity. As the network grows and more miners join the race to solve these puzzles, the competition becomes fiercer, requiring even more energy to secure the same amount of cryptocurrency.

The energy consumption of PoW is not linear—it scales with the number of miners. The more miners competing to solve the puzzle, the harder the puzzle becomes, leading to a continuous arms race of computing power. As miners race to solve these puzzles faster, they deploy larger and more powerful mining farms, which, in turn, require more energy to operate. This phenomenon has led to an explosion in energy use as **Bitcoin** and other PoW-based cryptocurrencies have grown in popularity.

In its early days, mining could be done on standard computers, with individuals able to mine from the comfort of their homes. But as the network expanded, mining became industrialized, with massive data centers filled with high-powered mining rigs working around the clock. These data centers are often located in regions where electricity is cheap, but not necessarily clean. This is especially true in places like China, where coal-powered energy is still prevalent.

The environmental impact of PoW becomes even clearer when considering how energy is sourced. A significant portion of mining operations rely on **non-renewable energy sources**, such as coal and natural gas, contributing to a considerable carbon footprint. While there are efforts to use renewable energy for mining, the sheer scale of energy consumption required for PoW makes it difficult for green energy alone to meet the demand. In some regions, miners take advantage of excess renewable energy—such as hydropower during wet seasons—but these efforts are not yet widespread enough to mitigate the overall impact.

Proof of Work's energy consumption, while central to its security model, presents a major challenge for sustainability. As we'll explore in the coming chapters, the search for more energy-efficient alternatives, like **Proof of Stake**, is critical if blockchain is to scale without devastating environmental consequences.

1.2: Bitcoin's Carbon Footprint: Beyond the Hype

Bitcoin, the first and most well-known cryptocurrency, has become synonymous with discussions about blockchain's environmental impact. Headlines often highlight how Bitcoin mining consumes more electricity than entire countries, and while these comparisons are attention-grabbing, they only tell part of the story. To fully understand Bitcoin's carbon footprint, we need to go beyond the hype and look at the specific factors driving its energy consumption.

The reason Bitcoin's energy use is so high lies in its reliance on the **Proof of Work (PoW)** consensus mechanism, which we explored earlier. In order to maintain its decentralized network, miners around the globe must compete to solve complex cryptographic puzzles, and the winner gets to add the next block to the blockchain, earning Bitcoin as a reward. This process, known as **mining**, is what consumes so much energy, especially as the competition for rewards has intensified.

As more miners join the network, the puzzles become harder, requiring more computational power to solve. This has led to a rapid increase in energy consumption over time. According to recent estimates, Bitcoin's annual energy usage is comparable to that of countries like Argentina and the Netherlands. While this figure can be startling, it's important to contextualize it. Bitcoin is not the only industry with a significant carbon footprint—many industries consume vast amounts of energy, from traditional banking systems to cloud computing and even gold mining. However, because Bitcoin operates in a decentralized manner, its energy consumption is more visible and often becomes the focal point in debates about sustainability.

Beyond the sheer amount of electricity used, another critical factor in Bitcoin's carbon footprint is the source of the energy. A large portion of Bitcoin mining is powered by non-renewable energy sources, such as **coal** and **natural gas**, particularly in regions like China and Kazakhstan, where energy costs are low but often come from carbon-heavy sources. The use of fossil fuels in Bitcoin mining is one of the primary reasons for its negative environmental image. Studies suggest that nearly 60-70% of Bitcoin mining's energy comes from nonrenewable sources, contributing to significant carbon emissions.

That said, it's important to note that not all Bitcoin mining is powered by dirty energy. Some miners have sought out regions with abundant **renewable energy** sources, such as **hydropower** in parts of China or **geothermal energy** in Iceland. In fact, certain studies have found that anywhere from 30-40% of Bitcoin's energy use comes from renewable sources, though these figures are often contested. What's clear is that there is potential for Bitcoin mining to shift towards greener energy, but for now, the majority of mining operations rely on cheap, non-renewable power.

Ultimately, Bitcoin's carbon footprint is a direct result of the PoW system, the scale of the network, and the energy sources miners choose to use. While the energy consumption is significant, it's essential to consider how other industries compare and what steps can be taken to reduce Bitcoin's reliance on non-renewable energy. As we'll explore in later chapters, alternatives to PoW and innovations like **carbon offset programs** may offer a path toward reducing Bitcoin's environmental impact.

1.3: Ethereum's Evolution: Gas Fees and Green Problems

Ethereum, the second-largest cryptocurrency by market capitalization, has played a pivotal role in expanding blockchain's use cases beyond digital currency. Its platform supports **smart contracts, decentralized applications (dApps)**, and **non-fungible tokens (NFTs)**, making it a crucial pillar in the blockchain ecosystem. However, with this expansion has come a significant environmental challenge. Like Bitcoin, Ethereum initially relied on the **Proof of Work (PoW)** consensus mechanism, resulting in substantial energy consumption, particularly during periods of high demand.

One unique aspect of Ethereum's environmental impact is tied to its transaction fees, known as **gas fees**. Gas fees are paid by users to miners to process and validate transactions on the network. The higher the demand for transactions, the higher the gas fees, as miners prioritize transactions with higher fees. During peak periods, such as the NFT boom of 2021, gas fees skyrocketed, leading to increased energy consumption as miners worked to validate as many transactions as possible to maximize profits. This dynamic, while driving network security, also escalated Ethereum's carbon footprint during periods of intense activity.

The environmental burden of Ethereum became even more apparent as its use cases expanded. The growth of **decentralized finance (DeFi)** applications, alongside the surge in NFT minting and trading, caused transaction volumes to soar. Each transaction required energy-intensive validation, contributing to a growing carbon footprint. As demand grew, so did the complexity of the cryptographic puzzles miners needed to solve, leading to even higher energy consumption.

Recognizing these issues, the Ethereum community began a long-awaited transition to a more sustainable model: **Proof of Stake (PoS)**. Unlike PoW, where miners compete based on computational power, PoS allows network validators to be selected based on the amount of cryptocurrency they hold and are willing to "stake" as collateral. This shift drastically reduces the energy requirements needed to secure the network, as the process no longer involves energy-hungry mining hardware.

The move to PoS, often referred to as **Ethereum 2.0**, represents a significant step toward reducing Ethereum's environmental impact. Initial estimates suggest that Ethereum's energy consumption could drop by over **99%** as a result of this transition, making it far more sustainable compared to its PoW predecessor. By shifting away from the mining model and embracing PoS, Ethereum is setting a new standard for environmental responsibility in blockchain technology.

However, it's worth noting that the environmental challenges Ethereum faced under the PoW system were not unique. Any blockchain relying on PoW will encounter similar issues as transaction volumes increase, leading to higher energy consumption.

What sets Ethereum apart is its willingness to evolve and address these concerns head-on. As Ethereum continues to transition fully into the PoS era, it offers a glimpse of how blockchain can be both innovative and environmentally sustainable.

1.4: The Numbers Don't Lie: Blockchain's Energy Consumption Data

When it comes to understanding the true environmental impact of blockchain technology, hard data is essential. The energy consumption of blockchain networks, particularly those relying on **Proof of Work (PoW)**, has become a focal point of criticism. To grasp the scale of the issue, it's crucial to compare blockchain's energy use with that of other industries and examine the sources of energy that miners rely on.

Estimates for **Bitcoin's energy consumption** vary slightly, but most data indicates that the network uses around **110 terawatt-hours (TWh)** of electricity annually. To put that in perspective, this is roughly the same amount of energy consumed by countries like **Argentina** or the **Netherlands** in a year. It's an enormous figure, especially considering that Bitcoin is just one of many blockchains operating today. This level of consumption raises critical questions about the long-term sustainability of blockchain technology if it continues to rely on energy-intensive processes.

Ethereum, prior to its transition to **Proof of Stake (PoS)**, consumed a similarly staggering amount of energy. At its peak, Ethereum's annual electricity consumption was estimated at around **72 TWh**, which is comparable to the energy usage of countries like **Austria** or **Colombia**. This was driven primarily by the network's demand for miners to validate transactions and execute smart contracts, a process that required substantial computational power.

However, comparing blockchain to entire nations can sometimes obscure more relevant industry comparisons. For example, **traditional banking** systems, which blockchain often seeks to replace or complement, are themselves energy-hungry. Maintaining global banking networks, from physical branches to data centers, consumes vast amounts of electricity. By some estimates, the traditional banking sector's energy consumption dwarfs that of blockchain, though these figures are often fragmented and harder to calculate due to the diffuse nature of the industry.

Another useful comparison is with the **gold mining** industry. Bitcoin is often referred to as "digital gold" due to its use as a store of value, and in many ways, the energy required to mine Bitcoin mirrors that of physical gold mining. Studies suggest that gold mining consumes approximately **240 TWh** annually, more than double the energy used by Bitcoin. While both industries have significant environmental impacts, it's worth noting that Bitcoin has the potential to become more energy-efficient through innovations like PoS, whereas physical gold mining will always require labor and machinery.

The energy source miners use is another critical component of blockchain's environmental impact. Much of the criticism aimed at Bitcoin and Ethereum stems from the fact that a large portion of their energy comes from **non-renewable sources**, particularly in regions like **Kazakhstan** and parts of **China**, where coal is a primary energy source. Mining operations in these regions contribute heavily to carbon emissions, exacerbating blockchain's environmental footprint.

That said, there is evidence that some mining operations are moving towards **renewable energy**. In certain regions, particularly in **Iceland** and **Canada**, miners are taking advantage of abundant renewable resources like **hydropower** and **geothermal energy**. Some studies suggest that up to **40%** of Bitcoin's energy consumption comes from renewable sources, though this number is highly contested.

Regardless, it's clear that where and how energy is sourced plays a crucial role in determining the overall environmental impact of blockchain networks.

The data doesn't lie—blockchain's energy consumption is substantial and cannot be ignored. However, as we've seen, these figures are not without context, and the industry is already moving toward more sustainable solutions. In the coming chapters, we'll explore the technological innovations and strategies being employed to reduce blockchain's carbon footprint and ensure that it can continue to scale without irreparably harming the environment.

While blockchain's energy consumption presents a formidable challenge, the real-world consequences of this environmental impact are even more sobering. From the strain on local ecosystems to the broader effects on global energy markets, the carbon footprint of blockchain extends far beyond the data centers that power it.

In the next chapter, we'll dive into how blockchain's energy demands are shaping our planet and the communities affected by its growth.

2. REAL-WORLD CONSEQUENCES: HOW BLOCKCHAIN IS SHAPING OUR PLANET

2.1: Mining Mayhem: Environmental Damage of Crypto Mining

The environmental consequences of cryptocurrency mining extend far beyond the energy consumption figures often cited in headlines. Mining operations, particularly those focused on **Proof of Work (PoW)** blockchains like Bitcoin, are not only energy-intensive but also cause significant damage to the local environment. From deforestation to the depletion of water resources, the physical impact of mining is a growing concern in regions where these operations are heavily concentrated.

One of the most visible environmental effects of large-scale mining operations is **deforestation**. In regions like **Inner Mongolia**, where mining facilities have flourished due to relatively cheap electricity, vast areas of land have been cleared to make room for data centers that house mining hardware. These facilities require significant infrastructure, not just for the mining machines themselves but also for cooling systems, power stations, and support buildings. The clearing of land for these purposes disrupts local ecosystems, displacing wildlife and contributing to the loss of biodiversity. The connection between mining and deforestation may not be immediately apparent, but the expansion of these operations has undoubtedly taken a toll on the environment.

Beyond deforestation, another major concern is the **water usage** associated with cryptocurrency mining, particularly in areas where water resources are already scarce. In regions like **China's Sichuan province**, where hydropower is abundant, miners rely heavily on rivers to generate electricity for their operations. While hydropower is often touted as a clean, renewable energy source, the massive scale of mining operations can strain local water supplies. In some cases, the diversion of water for energy production can reduce the availability of clean water for local communities, creating tensions between mining companies and residents. This issue is not limited to China—similar conflicts over water resources have arisen in parts of **Iceland** and the **United States**, where miners have set up operations to take advantage of renewable energy sources.

In addition to land and water usage, the sheer volume of **electronic waste** generated by cryptocurrency mining is another environmental problem. Mining requires the use of **ASICs (Application-Specific Integrated Circuits)**—highly specialized hardware designed solely for mining cryptocurrencies. These machines have a relatively short lifespan, as they quickly become obsolete when new, more efficient models are developed. As a result, millions of mining devices are discarded each year, contributing to the growing issue of e-waste. Unlike regular consumer electronics, ASICs cannot be repurposed or recycled easily, meaning that much of this waste ends up in landfills, where it releases harmful chemicals into the soil and water.

Moreover, mining facilities often require extensive **cooling systems** to prevent their hardware from overheating, especially in warmer climates. These cooling systems, which are energy-intensive in their own right, exacerbate the environmental impact of mining by increasing the overall electricity demand of the facility. In some cases, the heat generated by mining has been so significant that local ecosystems have been affected. For example, in certain areas, rivers used for hydropower cooling have experienced elevated temperatures, disrupting the natural habitat of fish and other aquatic species.

The environmental damage caused by mining is a direct result of the industry's need for constant, large-scale infrastructure. While the focus is often on the energy consumed by these operations, it's crucial to recognize the physical toll mining takes on the regions where it is concentrated. As mining expands, so too do the environmental consequences, creating a complex challenge for policymakers, environmentalists, and the blockchain industry itself. Finding ways to mitigate these impacts is essential if blockchain technology is to continue growing without irreversibly harming the planet's ecosystems.

2.2: The Global Carbon Footprint of Blockchain: Who's Paying the Price?

The carbon footprint of blockchain extends far beyond the localized environmental impacts of mining operations. On a global scale, the energy demands of blockchain technology are contributing to an increase in **greenhouse gas emissions**, influencing energy markets, and raising significant questions about the sustainability of its rapid growth. Understanding the broader implications of blockchain's carbon footprint requires looking at how its energy consumption contributes to global climate challenges.

Cryptocurrency mining, particularly in regions where **non-renewable energy sources** like coal are prevalent, has a significant carbon footprint. For example, in **Kazakhstan**, a major hub for Bitcoin mining due to its low energy costs, the vast majority of electricity is generated from coal-fired power plants. The result is a heavy reliance on fossil fuels to power mining operations, contributing to the country's overall carbon emissions and exacerbating global climate change. This is not unique to Kazakhstan—many mining operations worldwide are concentrated in areas where coal and natural gas are the primary sources of electricity.

The scale of emissions is staggering. Some studies suggest that **Bitcoin mining** alone contributes nearly **60 million tons of CO2** per year, roughly equivalent to the emissions of a small country like Greece. This figure continues to rise as the value and popularity of cryptocurrencies grow, drawing more miners into the network and increasing the energy required to maintain the blockchain. The **Proof of Work (PoW)** mechanism, while highly secure, is a key driver of this energy consumption, and as blockchain adoption grows, so too does its global carbon footprint.

One of the broader consequences of blockchain's energy demands is its impact on **global energy markets**. The growing appetite for electricity among miners has, in some cases, driven up energy prices in regions where mining is concentrated. In areas like **Texas**, where miners have flocked due to deregulated energy markets and abundant natural resources, the demand for electricity has spiked, leading to concerns about energy shortages and price surges for local residents. These issues are compounded during extreme weather events, such as the 2021 Texas freeze, where energy supplies were strained, and mining operations were temporarily halted due to widespread blackouts. The high energy demand of mining raises questions about how sustainable this industry can be if it continues to strain local and global energy grids.

In addition to influencing energy markets, blockchain's carbon footprint is increasingly coming under scrutiny from governments and regulatory bodies. As countries work to meet their **carbon reduction goals**, the environmental cost of cryptocurrency mining is becoming a key issue in climate policy discussions. Some countries, like **China**, have already implemented sweeping bans on cryptocurrency mining in part due to its environmental impact, while others are beginning to explore ways to regulate mining operations more closely. The European Union, for example, has been pushing for greater **energy efficiency** in digital technologies, with blockchain and cryptocurrency mining being key areas of focus.

The price of blockchain's carbon footprint is ultimately paid by everyone. As greenhouse gas emissions increase, so too do the impacts of **climate change**—rising global temperatures, more frequent extreme weather events, and shifts in ecosystems. While blockchain itself is not solely responsible for these issues, its energy demands add to the cumulative global challenge of reducing emissions and slowing climate change. The longer blockchain networks rely on non-renewable energy, the greater the impact on the planet.

Despite these challenges, the blockchain community is increasingly aware of its environmental responsibilities. As we'll explore in later chapters, efforts to **decarbonize** blockchain through renewable energy adoption, **carbon offset initiatives**, and alternative consensus mechanisms like **Proof of Stake (PoS)** are already underway. However, for these solutions to be effective, they need to be implemented on a global scale, with cooperation from governments, industry leaders, and the mining community itself. The future of blockchain depends on its ability to balance innovation with environmental sustainability, and addressing its global carbon footprint is a critical step in that journey.

2.3: Case Studies: Bitcoin vs. Ethereum vs. Smaller Chains

When it comes to blockchain's environmental impact, not all networks are created equal. **Bitcoin** and **Ethereum**, the two largest cryptocurrencies, have dominated the conversation due to their immense popularity and substantial energy consumption, but there are also smaller blockchain networks that operate with significantly less impact. Understanding the environmental differences between these networks provides insight into where the industry is headed and how new technologies might mitigate the problems associated with energy-intensive blockchains.

Bitcoin, as the first and most valuable cryptocurrency, is also one of the most energy-hungry. Its **Proof of Work (PoW)** consensus mechanism, which secures the network, requires massive computational resources. As discussed earlier, Bitcoin mining operations are responsible for consuming more energy than some small countries, and much of this energy comes from non-renewable sources. Bitcoin's simplicity—it was designed purely as a decentralized digital currency—means there's little flexibility within its protocol to transition away from PoW. As such, any reduction in Bitcoin's environmental impact will likely need to come from external factors, such as miners switching to **renewable energy** or adopting **carbon offset initiatives**.

Ethereum, on the other hand, presents a more dynamic case. Like Bitcoin, Ethereum originally relied on PoW, leading to substantial energy consumption, especially as the network grew to support decentralized applications (dApps), **DeFi (Decentralized Finance)** projects, and **NFTs** (non-fungible tokens). However, Ethereum's transition to **Proof of Stake (PoS)** through **Ethereum 2.0** marks a significant shift. With PoS, validators are chosen based on the amount of cryptocurrency they hold and are willing to "stake" as collateral, eliminating the need for energy-intensive mining operations. This transition has dramatically reduced Ethereum's carbon footprint, with estimates suggesting a **99%** decrease in energy consumption. Ethereum's evolution shows that even large, established networks can embrace more sustainable practices, setting a new standard for the industry.

The contrast between Bitcoin and Ethereum is stark, but there are also smaller blockchain networks that have prioritized environmental sustainability from the start. One example is **Tezos**, a blockchain that has used PoS since its inception. Tezos is known for its energy efficiency, consuming far less electricity than PoW-based networks while still maintaining a high level of security and decentralization. Similarly, **Algorand** is another PoS-based blockchain that has made environmental sustainability a core part of its mission. Algorand's leadership has committed to offsetting the network's carbon emissions, making it one of the most eco-friendly blockchains in operation.

There are also hybrid approaches like **Polkadot**, which uses a **Nominated Proof of Stake (NPoS)** consensus mechanism to reduce energy consumption while maintaining scalability and security. Polkadot's modular design allows for various blockchains, or "parachains," to operate within its ecosystem, each optimized for different use cases. This flexibility enables more efficient resource allocation, which reduces the overall environmental impact of the network.

In comparing these case studies, it's clear that **consensus mechanisms** play a crucial role in determining the energy consumption of a blockchain network. PoW networks like Bitcoin are inherently more energy-intensive due to the competitive nature of mining, while PoS and other alternative mechanisms offer much more energy-efficient solutions. As more blockchain projects adopt PoS or explore new consensus models, the overall environmental impact of the industry is likely to decrease, provided that these innovations are implemented on a broad scale.

Looking at these case studies, it's evident that the future of blockchain will depend on continued innovation and the willingness of networks to evolve. Ethereum's transition to PoS demonstrates that even the largest players in the space can take steps toward sustainability, while newer projects like Tezos and Algorand are proving that it's possible to build environmentally friendly blockchain networks from the ground up. Bitcoin, while currently stuck with PoW, may also see advancements through the increased use of renewable energy or other creative solutions to reduce its carbon footprint. The key takeaway is that blockchain's environmental impact is not uniform, and by examining these case studies, we can better understand the pathways toward a more sustainable future for the industry.

2.4: Societal Impact: Energy Strains on Developing Nations

One of the lesser-discussed but increasingly important aspects of blockchain's environmental impact is how it affects **developing nations**, particularly those with underdeveloped energy infrastructures. As cryptocurrency mining operations expand into regions where electricity is cheap but scarce, the strain on local resources can create significant challenges for both governments and citizens. The **socioeconomic implications** of energy-hungry mining operations often hit hardest in these vulnerable areas, where the promise of economic growth from blockchain technology can sometimes lead to unintended consequences.

Developing nations are often attractive destinations for cryptocurrency miners due to their lower electricity costs. These regions can offer cheaper energy for large-scale mining farms, often because of government subsidies or an abundance of natural resources. However, these benefits come at a cost. In many developing countries, the local power grid is not built to handle the sudden spike in electricity demand that large mining operations require. This increased demand can lead to **power outages** and energy shortages, leaving local communities without reliable access to electricity for basic needs like lighting, cooking, and heating.

One such example is **Iran**, which became a hotspot for cryptocurrency mining in the mid-2010s due to its heavily subsidized energy prices. The country's cheap electricity attracted miners from across the globe, leading to the establishment of large-scale mining operations. However, as the demand for energy grew, Iran's aging energy infrastructure struggled to keep up. In 2021, widespread **blackouts** affected millions of people, and mining operations were identified as a significant contributing factor. The Iranian government eventually imposed temporary bans on mining to alleviate pressure on the energy grid, but the damage to the local population had already been done.

Similarly, in **Kazakhstan**, which became one of the world's leading mining hubs after China's crackdown on cryptocurrency mining, the energy grid has been under immense strain. While mining brought an influx of investment to Kazakhstan, the country's coal-dependent energy sector couldn't keep up with the demand. This has led to power shortages that have impacted not just miners but also households and businesses. In response, Kazakhstan has been forced to import electricity from neighboring countries, further complicating the situation and raising energy prices for local citizens.

The social implications of these energy strains are profound. In regions where energy is already scarce or expensive, the arrival of large mining operations can exacerbate existing inequalities. When the energy grid is stretched beyond capacity, it's often the local populations, particularly those in rural areas, who suffer the most. They may experience more frequent power cuts, higher energy bills, or even lose access to electricity altogether. For communities that already face challenges related to poverty and underdevelopment, these disruptions can have far-reaching consequences, including a negative impact on **education, healthcare**, and local **economic stability**.

In addition to energy shortages, mining operations can also lead to environmental degradation in developing countries, particularly where regulations are weak or enforcement is limited. In regions where **hydropower** is abundant, miners often build facilities near rivers or lakes, diverting water resources to generate electricity. This can reduce water availability for local agriculture and drinking water supplies, placing additional strain on already fragile ecosystems. Without strict environmental protections in place, the long-term effects of these operations can be devastating for both the environment and the communities that depend on it.

Despite these challenges, there are also opportunities for developing nations to harness the power of blockchain technology in a more sustainable and equitable way. Some governments are exploring ways to **regulate** cryptocurrency mining more effectively, ensuring that operations contribute positively to the local economy without overburdening the energy grid. Others are looking at ways to incentivize the use of **renewable energy** for mining operations, which could help reduce the environmental and social impact of the industry. For example, **El Salvador**, the first country to adopt Bitcoin as legal tender, has announced plans to power its mining operations using **geothermal energy** from its volcanoes, a renewable resource that could help offset the country's reliance on fossil fuels.

As cryptocurrency continues to grow in popularity, the societal impact of its energy consumption will become an increasingly pressing issue for developing nations. Governments will need to balance the potential economic benefits of attracting mining operations with the need to protect their energy infrastructure and the wellbeing of their citizens. If left unchecked, the energy strains created by cryptocurrency mining could widen existing inequalities and contribute to further environmental degradation. However, with the right regulations and a focus on sustainable energy, it is possible for developing nations to benefit from blockchain technology without sacrificing the needs of their populations.

The environmental and societal costs of blockchain are undeniable, particularly in developing nations where energy shortages and infrastructure challenges are most keenly felt. However, while these consequences are severe, they are not insurmountable. The blockchain industry is beginning to recognize the need for change, with innovators exploring sustainable solutions that could transform how these technologies operate.

In the next chapter, we will delve into the promising developments that are leading the charge toward greener blockchain networks, examining how alternative consensus mechanisms and forward-thinking initiatives are shaping a more sustainable future for the technology.

3. GREENER PASTURES: SUSTAINABLE SOLUTIONS FOR BLOCKCHAIN

3.1: Proof of Stake: A More Sustainable Consensus Mechanism?

As the environmental impact of **Proof of Work (PoW)** becomes more widely recognized, blockchain developers and communities have been actively seeking alternatives to reduce energy consumption. One of the most promising and widely discussed alternatives is **Proof of Stake (PoS)**, a consensus mechanism that dramatically decreases the need for energy-intensive computational processes. Unlike PoW, which relies on miners competing to solve complex puzzles, PoS selects validators based on the amount of cryptocurrency they hold and are willing to "stake" as collateral. This fundamental difference results in significantly lower energy usage while maintaining the network's security and decentralization.

In PoS, the energy consumption issue that plagues PoW is virtually eliminated because there is no need for miners to constantly run powerful hardware to validate transactions. Instead, network participants, known as **validators**, are selected in proportion to the amount of cryptocurrency they have staked in the network. This process doesn't require vast computational resources, meaning PoS-based blockchains can function with a fraction of the energy that PoW systems demand. Studies suggest that **Ethereum's** switch to PoS could result in a **99% reduction** in its energy consumption, showcasing just how significant the difference between these two mechanisms can be.

The **environmental benefits** of PoS go beyond energy savings. By reducing the need for mining farms and power-hungry data centers, PoS minimizes the physical infrastructure required to sustain a blockchain. This means fewer facilities consuming electricity from fossil fuels, fewer electronic devices contributing to e-waste, and less pressure on local energy grids in regions where mining had previously dominated. Moreover, because PoS networks don't require constant hardware upgrades to remain competitive, the **lifespan of equipment** used by validators is longer, further reducing the waste generated by obsolete technology.

Ethereum's transition to PoS, known as Ethereum 2.0, is one of the most prominent examples of how the blockchain community is embracing more sustainable practices. This transition marks a watershed moment in the industry, as Ethereum was previously the second-largest consumer of energy among cryptocurrencies due to its PoW system. By moving to PoS, Ethereum is setting a precedent for other blockchain networks to follow. While some critics argue that PoS introduces centralization risks, with wealthier validators having more influence over the network, the energy savings and environmental benefits are undeniable.

Other blockchain projects, such as **Cardano**, **Polkadot**, and **Tezos**, have implemented PoS from the start, positioning themselves as environmentally conscious alternatives to PoW-heavy networks like Bitcoin. These projects not only benefit from reduced energy consumption but also contribute to the growing narrative that blockchain technology can be both innovative and sustainable. With major platforms like Ethereum making the switch to PoS, the trend toward greener blockchain technology is gaining momentum.

However, PoS is not without its challenges. One of the primary concerns is the **initial distribution of wealth**, as validators must hold a significant amount of cryptocurrency to participate in securing the network. This could potentially lead to centralization, where only a few large stakeholders control the validation process. Nonetheless, ongoing research and development within the blockchain community are focused on addressing these concerns and improving the robustness of PoS systems.

As more blockchain networks adopt PoS or other energy-efficient alternatives, the overall environmental impact of the industry is expected to decrease significantly. The shift away from PoW represents a critical turning point for blockchain technology, as it demonstrates that the industry can innovate while addressing its environmental responsibilities.

3.2: Layer 2: Scaling Solutions and Their Eco-Impact

As blockchain networks grow and transaction volumes increase, scalability has become one of the most pressing issues for developers. The more popular a blockchain becomes, the more computational resources are required to validate transactions, which in turn drives up energy consumption. **Layer 2 solutions** have emerged as a key method to address both scalability and energy efficiency by reducing the burden on the main blockchain (Layer 1) without compromising security or decentralization.

Layer 2 solutions are protocols built on top of the main blockchain that handle transactions off-chain, reducing the need for every transaction to be recorded and validated directly on the core network. Once a batch of transactions has been processed, only the final result is submitted to the main blockchain, significantly lowering the computational effort required to secure the network. By offloading the bulk of transactional work to Layer 2, these solutions dramatically cut the energy needed for transaction validation.

One of the most well-known Layer 2 solutions is the **Lightning Network**, designed to improve the scalability of **Bitcoin**. The Lightning Network enables users to open off-chain payment channels where multiple transactions can take place without directly interacting with the Bitcoin blockchain. Once the channel is closed, only the final state of the transactions is recorded on-chain, meaning the vast majority of the network's energy-intensive mining resources are not required for every individual transaction. This significantly reduces Bitcoin's energy consumption while allowing for faster and cheaper transactions, making it more efficient without compromising its decentralized nature.

Ethereum has also embraced Layer 2 solutions, with **Optimistic Rollups** and **ZK-Rollups** playing a crucial role in its scaling strategy. Rollups bundle transactions together off-chain and submit them to the Ethereum blockchain as a single batch. This approach not only reduces the amount of data processed on the main network but also cuts down on the energy required for each individual transaction. These solutions are particularly important for Ethereum, given its history of high **gas fees** and energy consumption during periods of heavy usage, such as the **NFT** and **DeFi** booms. By implementing Layer 2 scaling solutions, Ethereum is significantly reducing its environmental footprint while still enabling the vast array of decentralized applications that rely on its network.

Another advantage of Layer 2 solutions is their ability to reduce **congestion** on the main blockchain, which further lowers energy consumption. When blockchains become congested with too many transactions, the network must work harder, consuming more energy to maintain its operations. By moving transactions off-chain, Layer 2 solutions alleviate this congestion, leading to more efficient energy use. This becomes particularly valuable for networks like Bitcoin and Ethereum, where spikes in transaction volume can result in significant energy consumption increases.

In addition to reducing energy use, Layer 2 solutions also contribute to improving **transaction throughput**, which can make blockchain networks more appealing for everyday use. This scalability improvement could drive further adoption of blockchain technology in areas like payments, gaming, and supply chain management, all while ensuring that the environmental impact remains minimized. The growing adoption of Layer 2 solutions represents a significant step forward for the blockchain industry, showing that it is possible to maintain decentralized networks without the excessive energy consumption traditionally associated with **Proof of Work (PoW)** blockchains.

As more blockchain projects explore Layer 2 solutions, the potential for reducing the environmental impact of blockchain technology becomes more tangible. These innovations are not only making blockchain networks more efficient and scalable but are also positioning the industry as a whole to move toward a more sustainable future. The implementation of Layer 2 protocols, combined with other green initiatives, will play a crucial role in transforming blockchain from an energy-intensive technology into one that can scale responsibly.

3.3: Sidechains, Sharding, and Beyond: Efficiency in Practice

In addition to **Layer 2 solutions**, other scalability innovations are emerging that can further reduce blockchain's environmental impact. Two of the most prominent techniques in this area are **sidechains** and **sharding**, both of which aim to increase the efficiency of blockchain networks by distributing the workload in a more manageable and energy-efficient way. These methods, while distinct from Layer 2 solutions, provide an alternative approach to addressing the energy and scalability challenges faced by blockchain networks, especially those still reliant on **Proof of Work (PoW)**.

Sidechains are independent blockchain networks that run parallel to the main blockchain (often referred to as the **parent chain**). Transactions can be processed on the sidechain, and the final result is recorded on the parent chain once the sidechain completes its work. This allows for more flexibility and reduces congestion on the main network, similar to how Layer 2 solutions operate. However, sidechains differ in that they have their own set of rules, consensus mechanisms, and security protocols. One of the key advantages of sidechains is that they can be optimized for specific use cases, such as **faster transaction speeds**, **lower fees**, or **enhanced privacy**, without burdening the main network with every transaction.

A well-known example of a sidechain implementation is **Polygon**, which operates alongside **Ethereum**. Polygon allows for faster and more energy-efficient transactions by processing them on its sidechain and then securing the final result on Ethereum. This not only reduces the energy consumption of each transaction but also alleviates some of the congestion issues that Ethereum has historically faced. By utilizing sidechains, Ethereum can scale to handle more applications and users without significantly increasing its environmental footprint. The separation of tasks between the main chain and the sidechain leads to a more efficient use of computational resources, directly impacting energy consumption in a positive way.

Another groundbreaking solution is **sharding**, which divides the blockchain into smaller, manageable pieces, known as **shards**. Each shard operates independently and processes a portion of the network's transactions, allowing multiple transactions to be processed in parallel rather than sequentially. This approach dramatically increases the throughput of the blockchain, as each shard can handle its own workload, reducing the computational burden on the entire network. Sharding not only enhances performance but also minimizes the amount of energy required for each transaction by distributing the work across multiple nodes.

Ethereum 2.0 plans to incorporate sharding as part of its transition to a **Proof of Stake (PoS)** consensus mechanism. By splitting the network into 64 shards, Ethereum aims to increase its scalability while reducing the energy consumption associated with processing transactions. Sharding allows Ethereum to process a much higher number of transactions per second, making it more efficient and sustainable. Other blockchains, such as **Zilliqa**, have already implemented sharding with notable success, demonstrating that this technique can significantly improve both scalability and energy efficiency.

Beyond these two techniques, there are additional innovations being developed to optimize blockchain's energy usage. Some projects are experimenting with **hybrid consensus mechanisms**, which combine elements of PoW and PoS to strike a balance between security and energy efficiency. Others are exploring ways to integrate **machine learning** algorithms to further optimize how resources are allocated within the network, ensuring that energy is used only when absolutely necessary. These efforts are part of a broader push within the blockchain community to rethink how blockchain systems are built, with an eye toward sustainability and long-term viability.

While sidechains, sharding, and hybrid models offer promising solutions to blockchain's scalability and energy challenges, it's important to recognize that these technologies are still in the early stages of adoption. However, as more blockchain projects implement these innovations, the overall environmental impact of the industry is likely to decrease. These approaches demonstrate that scalability and sustainability are not mutually exclusive; with the right technology in place, blockchain can evolve to meet growing demand without causing significant environmental harm.

By reducing the computational load on the main blockchain, these innovations not only improve transaction throughput but also ensure that the energy required to run the network is used more efficiently. As blockchain continues to expand, the implementation of sidechains, sharding, and other efficiency-driven solutions will be crucial to minimizing its environmental footprint while maintaining the decentralized nature that makes blockchain so revolutionary.

3.4: Green Initiatives: Carbon Offset Programs and Blockchain's Environmental Projects

As awareness of blockchain's environmental impact grows, the industry is beginning to embrace **green initiatives** aimed at reducing or offsetting its carbon footprint. These efforts include everything from direct **carbon offset programs** to innovative projects that leverage blockchain technology to promote environmental sustainability. The adoption of these initiatives marks an important step toward making blockchain a more eco-friendly industry while still preserving its decentralized nature.

One of the most widely used approaches to addressing blockchain's carbon footprint is through **carbon offset programs**. These programs allow companies and individuals to compensate for their carbon emissions by funding projects that reduce or remove CO_2 from the atmosphere. For example, some blockchain networks and companies are purchasing **carbon credits**, which represent a reduction of one ton of carbon dioxide emissions. By investing in carbon offset projects, such as reforestation, renewable energy, or carbon capture technology, these companies can effectively neutralize the emissions generated by their mining operations or other blockchain-related activities.

Chia Network, a blockchain project that has been marketed as a "green" alternative to **Proof of Work (PoW)** systems, is an example of how carbon offsetting is being integrated into the blockchain space. Chia uses a unique consensus mechanism known as **Proof of Space and Time**, which relies on unused hard drive space rather than energy-intensive computational power. The network is not only more energy-efficient than traditional PoW systems but has also made efforts to offset its remaining emissions through carbon credits. Chia's leadership has emphasized the importance of minimizing the environmental impact of blockchain technology from the ground up, setting an example for how blockchain can incorporate green practices.

Beyond offsetting carbon emissions, blockchain technology is being used to promote **renewable energy** projects. Platforms like **Power Ledger** are leveraging blockchain's transparency and security to create decentralized energy markets, where users can buy and sell renewable energy directly. Power Ledger's system tracks energy production and consumption in real-time, ensuring that energy transactions are transparent and verifiable. This application of blockchain not only promotes the use of renewable energy but also demonstrates how blockchain can be part of the solution to the global energy crisis, rather than contributing to the problem.

Another promising initiative is the use of blockchain to track **supply chain sustainability**. Companies and organizations are increasingly using blockchain to ensure that their supply chains are environmentally friendly, transparent, and ethical. Blockchain's immutable ledger allows for real-time tracking of materials, products, and resources, ensuring that every step of the process adheres to strict environmental standards. This technology has already been used in industries like agriculture, mining, and manufacturing, where sustainability is often difficult to verify through traditional means. By using blockchain to hold companies accountable, these projects are helping to reduce the environmental impact of various industries, from food production to fashion.

One of the most exciting uses of blockchain in environmental sustainability is its role in promoting **decentralized finance (DeFi)** projects that support green initiatives. Some blockchain-based platforms are creating decentralized ecosystems where users can invest in environmentally focused projects, such as renewable energy startups, carbon capture technology, and sustainable agriculture. These platforms offer users the ability to invest in green projects while also benefiting from the transparency and efficiency of blockchain technology. By democratizing access to green investments, DeFi platforms have the potential to scale environmentally friendly projects that may otherwise struggle to secure funding.

As blockchain technology evolves, the adoption of **green initiatives** will likely become more widespread. While blockchain's environmental challenges are significant, the industry is increasingly recognizing the need to address these issues head-on. From carbon offset programs to renewable energy markets, blockchain has the potential to transform not only how energy is consumed but also how it is produced and distributed. By focusing on sustainability, the blockchain community can ensure that its innovations contribute to solving the world's environmental challenges rather than exacerbating them.

These green initiatives demonstrate that blockchain can be part of the solution to the environmental problems it currently faces. While the industry has a long way to go in terms of reducing its overall carbon footprint, the growing number of environmentally focused projects shows that blockchain's future can be greener. As blockchain continues to expand, the development and adoption of these initiatives will play a crucial role in shaping the technology's impact on the environment.

Blockchain's journey towards environmental sustainability is ongoing, with innovative solutions like **Proof of Stake**, **Layer 2 scaling**, **sidechains**, and **carbon offset programs** making significant strides. These efforts are beginning to reshape the narrative around blockchain's energy consumption, showing that with the right technologies and initiatives, the industry can drastically reduce its environmental footprint. The growing adoption of these green technologies highlights the potential for blockchain to evolve into a more eco-conscious industry, one that balances innovation with sustainability.

However, these solutions are only part of the equation. The future of blockchain's environmental impact depends not just on technology, but also on the regulatory frameworks, market forces, and societal shifts that influence how and where blockchain operates.

In the next chapter, we will explore the future of blockchain's environmental impact, diving into emerging technologies and regulatory efforts that aim to address the challenges posed by blockchain's growth, while ensuring that its evolution remains sustainable and aligned with global environmental goals.

4. THE FUTURE OF BLOCKCHAIN'S ENVIRONMENTAL IMPACT

4.1: What's on the Horizon: New Tech & Green Innovation

The future of blockchain is closely tied to the ongoing development of new technologies designed to make the industry more energy-efficient and sustainable. With **Proof of Stake (PoS)** now a well-established alternative to the energy-hungry **Proof of Work (PoW)**, innovators are pushing the boundaries of blockchain's potential even further. Some of the most promising advancements include **Proof of Space and Time, zero-knowledge proofs**, and the potential game-changing implications of **quantum computing**. These technologies not only offer improvements in energy efficiency but could also reshape the way blockchain networks operate in the coming years.

One of the most exciting breakthroughs in blockchain is the use of **Proof of Space and Time (PoST)**, a consensus mechanism used by the **Chia Network**. Unlike PoW, which requires miners to solve complex mathematical problems using large amounts of computational power, PoST uses unused hard drive space to secure the network. Users allocate storage space on their drives, and the system relies on both the space and the passage of time to verify and validate blocks. This drastically reduces the energy consumption required to maintain the blockchain, as hard drives consume far less power than traditional mining hardware. Chia has positioned itself as an environmentally friendly alternative to PoW systems, emphasizing sustainability while maintaining the security of the network. With growing interest in this model, PoST could become a key component of future blockchain networks.

In addition to PoST, **zero-knowledge proofs (ZKPs)** are another groundbreaking innovation with the potential to reduce blockchain's environmental impact. ZKPs are cryptographic tools that allow one party to prove to another that a statement is true without revealing the underlying data. By reducing the amount of data that needs to be processed on-chain, ZKPs can lower the computational requirements for verifying transactions. This, in turn, decreases the overall energy consumption of the network. **Zcash**, a privacy-focused cryptocurrency, has already integrated ZKPs to enhance both privacy and efficiency, demonstrating the potential of these proofs to streamline blockchain processes. As more blockchain networks adopt ZKPs, we can expect to see a reduction in the amount of energy needed to maintain decentralized systems.

Looking further into the future, **quantum computing** could have a profound impact on the blockchain industry, both in terms of efficiency and security. While still in the experimental phase, quantum computers are capable of processing information at speeds far beyond that of classical computers. This increased processing power could be used to dramatically reduce the energy required for cryptographic tasks, such as verifying transactions or securing networks. However, quantum computing also presents challenges for blockchain, as current encryption methods may become vulnerable to quantum attacks. Researchers are already exploring **quantum-resistant cryptography** to ensure that blockchain systems remain secure in a post-quantum world. If quantum computing becomes widely accessible, it could revolutionize blockchain technology by making it faster, more secure, and far more energy-efficient than today's systems.

These emerging technologies represent just a fraction of the potential advancements that could transform blockchain's environmental impact. With continued innovation and investment in energy-efficient solutions, the blockchain industry is poised to evolve into a more sustainable and responsible sector. The key to success will be in the broad adoption of these new technologies, as well as the collaboration between developers, policymakers, and environmental advocates to ensure that blockchain's growth aligns with global sustainability goals. The road ahead is filled with challenges, but the technologies on the horizon offer a promising path toward a greener future for blockchain.

4.2: Governance and Regulation: Can Policy Shape Blockchain's Future?

As blockchain technology continues to evolve, the role of **government regulation** and **policy frameworks** in shaping its environmental impact is becoming increasingly important. While technological innovation is essential in reducing energy consumption, regulatory oversight plays a crucial role in ensuring that blockchain networks are held accountable for their carbon footprint. The challenge for governments and global regulatory bodies is to balance the promotion of innovation with the enforcement of environmental responsibility. As climate change becomes a global priority, policies aimed at reducing blockchain's environmental impact are beginning to take shape, and their influence will be vital in determining the future of the industry.

One of the most significant regulatory trends is the push for **carbon taxation** on energy-intensive industries, including cryptocurrency mining. Carbon taxes place a monetary cost on emissions, incentivizing businesses to reduce their carbon footprint. In the context of blockchain, countries that host large-scale mining operations, such as **Kazakhstan** and the **United States**, are considering the implementation of carbon taxes specifically targeted at cryptocurrency miners. By making it more expensive to mine using non-renewable energy sources, these taxes aim to shift miners towards greener alternatives. However, the success of such policies will depend on how they are implemented and whether miners have access to affordable renewable energy sources in these regions.
In addition to taxation, some governments are exploring the development of **green crypto standards**. These standards would set guidelines for blockchain networks to meet certain environmental criteria, such as using renewable energy, minimizing electronic

waste, and reducing energy consumption. In **Europe**, regulatory discussions around green crypto standards are gaining traction as part of the European Union's broader **Green Deal** initiative, which seeks to achieve climate neutrality by 2050. If adopted, these standards could pave the way for a new generation of blockchain networks designed with sustainability in mind from the start. Similarly, organizations like the **Crypto Climate Accord** are advocating for the industry to achieve net-zero emissions by 2030, offering a voluntary framework for blockchain companies to commit to environmental responsibility.

Another important factor in the regulatory landscape is the role of **global regulatory bodies** and international cooperation. Blockchain is inherently decentralized and often operates across borders, making it difficult for any one country to regulate effectively. As a result, international organizations, such as the **United Nations Framework Convention on Climate Change (UNFCCC)**, are beginning to engage with blockchain's environmental challenges at a global level. These bodies are well-positioned to establish international standards and facilitate cooperation between countries, ensuring that the environmental impact of blockchain is addressed on a global scale. Collaborative efforts could include carbon offset requirements for blockchain projects or the development of renewable energy infrastructure to support mining operations.

However, regulation is not without its challenges. Overly restrictive policies could stifle innovation in the blockchain space, driving companies to move their operations to regions with lax environmental standards. This **regulatory arbitrage** is already a concern, as some mining operations have migrated from regions like **China**, where mining was banned, to countries with fewer restrictions on energy consumption. This highlights the need for a balanced approach that encourages sustainability while allowing blockchain technology to continue evolving.

Ultimately, the future of blockchain's environmental impact will be shaped not only by technological advancements but also by the policies and regulations that govern the industry. Governments and regulatory bodies will need to work in tandem with developers and environmental advocates to create a framework that promotes innovation while addressing the urgent need for environmental sustainability. As blockchain continues to grow, policy will play a crucial role in steering the industry toward greener practices, ensuring that its development aligns with global efforts to combat climate change.

4.3: From Data Centers to Decentralization: Infrastructure Overhauls

Blockchain's environmental impact is closely tied to the physical infrastructure required to support its networks. The vast data centers that power **Proof of Work (PoW)** mining operations, with their relentless energy demands, have long been a focal point in discussions about sustainability. However, the infrastructure supporting blockchain is evolving rapidly, and efforts to overhaul how data centers operate—combined with decentralization—could transform blockchain's environmental footprint in the coming years.

The energy consumption of **data centers** has skyrocketed as blockchain networks have grown, particularly those relying on PoW mechanisms. These facilities house the hardware necessary for mining and transaction validation, generating massive energy demand due to the need for constant power and cooling. Improving the **energy efficiency** of these data centers is essential in reducing blockchain's environmental impact. A growing number of mining operations are beginning to integrate **renewable energy sources** into their data centers to offset their energy consumption. In countries like **Iceland**, for instance, mining companies are taking advantage of the region's abundant **geothermal energy** to power their operations, dramatically reducing their carbon footprint. Similarly, in **Canada**, hydropower is being used to support mining facilities, offering a cleaner alternative to coal and natural gas.

Moreover, advances in **data center design** are helping to improve overall energy efficiency. Modern data centers are incorporating **liquid cooling systems** and other technologies to reduce the amount of energy needed to cool servers, minimizing waste. These infrastructure innovations are not only reducing the environmental burden of blockchain but also setting new standards for how data centers across industries can operate more sustainably.

Alongside improvements in data center efficiency, the concept of **decentralized energy grids** is gaining traction. Blockchain's decentralized nature means that mining and validation operations can be spread out globally, which opens the door for a more distributed approach to energy consumption. Decentralized energy grids would enable miners and validators to access local renewable energy sources directly, reducing the need for large-scale data centers that draw power from non-renewable energy sources. Projects like **Energy Web** are already exploring how blockchain can be used to create decentralized, community-based energy grids, empowering individuals and businesses to participate in energy production and consumption in a more sustainable way.

Another important development is the shift toward smaller, more **distributed nodes** in blockchain networks. Historically, mining has been concentrated in a few large-scale operations, but there is a growing movement toward decentralizing these efforts by spreading out computational power among smaller nodes. This shift reduces the concentration of energy usage in specific regions, lowering the overall environmental strain. By distributing validation across more nodes, blockchain networks can improve their energy efficiency while maintaining security and decentralization.

The drive to decentralize blockchain infrastructure also extends beyond energy concerns. Smaller, distributed nodes offer the potential for more resilient networks that are less vulnerable to attacks or failures, reinforcing blockchain's promise of decentralized security. As blockchain infrastructure continues to evolve, the push toward decentralization and renewable energy adoption is likely to reshape the way data centers operate, moving the industry toward a more sustainable model. The combination of data center innovation, decentralized energy grids, and distributed nodes offers a promising path forward for reducing blockchain's environmental impact.

4.4: Thought Leader Perspectives: The Next Steps in Blockchain Sustainability

Blockchain's environmental future is a topic that has captured the attention of researchers, developers, and industry leaders alike. As the push for greener technologies accelerates, thought leaders in the blockchain space are increasingly focusing on how to balance the power of decentralized systems with sustainability goals. Insights from those at the forefront of blockchain development highlight the challenges and opportunities ahead for creating a truly sustainable blockchain ecosystem.

One of the most vocal proponents of sustainability in blockchain is **Vitalik Buterin**, the co-founder of Ethereum. Buterin has long emphasized the importance of transitioning away from **Proof of Work (PoW)** toward more energy-efficient consensus mechanisms like **Proof of Stake (PoS)**, a shift that Ethereum has embraced with its **Ethereum 2.0** upgrade. Buterin believes that PoS not only makes blockchain more environmentally friendly but also opens the door for future innovations that could further reduce the industry's energy consumption. His advocacy for PoS has sparked widespread discussion about whether other major blockchain networks, such as Bitcoin, should consider similar transitions to improve their sustainability profiles.

Another influential voice is **Leah Callon-Butler**, a blockchain sustainability consultant and writer. She has pointed out the growing need for the blockchain industry to take a leadership role in **green finance** and **sustainable development goals** (SDGs). Callon-Butler has been a strong advocate for using blockchain to promote transparency in carbon markets, where decentralized systems can help verify carbon offsets and ensure that environmental goals are being met. Her work highlights the potential for blockchain to support not just its own sustainability goals, but also broader global efforts to mitigate climate change through transparent and verifiable solutions.

Kathleen Breitman, co-founder of **Tezos**, has also championed the idea that blockchain technology can lead by example in adopting **green practices**. Tezos, which has used PoS from its inception, is one of the blockchain platforms with a much smaller energy footprint compared to PoW networks. Breitman has been an advocate for exploring blockchain's potential beyond financial transactions, especially in sectors like energy and sustainability. By providing efficient, decentralized platforms, Tezos and other PoS networks are helping to demonstrate that blockchain can offer scalable solutions while minimizing environmental harm.

There are also emerging leaders in the **regenerative finance (ReFi)** space, which focuses on aligning financial incentives with environmental goals. Projects like **KlimaDAO** are pushing the boundaries of how blockchain can be used to combat climate change directly. Through tokenized carbon credits and a decentralized market for carbon trading, KlimaDAO aims to create economic incentives for individuals and organizations to offset their carbon emissions. These thought leaders believe that by connecting blockchain with climate action, it is possible to create a sustainable economy that benefits both the planet and blockchain users.

Looking to the future, industry experts agree that collaboration between developers, policymakers, and environmental advocates will be crucial for ensuring that blockchain can scale without exacerbating global energy issues. Thought leaders in blockchain recognize that the path forward involves more than just technological advancements—it requires a concerted effort to incorporate sustainable practices at every level of the blockchain ecosystem.

By focusing on solutions that go beyond energy consumption, such as transparency in supply chains, carbon offset tracking, and decentralized energy systems, blockchain innovators are proving that sustainability and technology are not mutually exclusive. Thought leaders are helping to shape a narrative that blockchain can be a force for good in the fight against climate change, provided the right strategies and innovations are put into place.

The future of blockchain's environmental impact lies at the intersection of technological innovation, policy change, and industry-wide collaboration. As we've seen, advances like **Proof of Stake (PoS)**, **Layer 2 scaling**, and **sidechains** are already making significant strides in reducing blockchain's energy consumption. At the same time, the role of governance and regulation will become increasingly critical in ensuring that blockchain's growth aligns with global sustainability goals. Insights from industry leaders point to the vast potential for blockchain to not only minimize its environmental footprint but to also contribute to broader climate initiatives, such as through carbon trading and decentralized energy solutions.

As blockchain continues to evolve, it is clear that the environmental challenges it poses are not insurmountable. With the right technologies and regulatory frameworks in place, the industry is poised to become a leader in sustainable innovation.

In the next chapter, we will take a closer look at the **actionable steps** individuals and organizations can take to engage with eco-friendly blockchain solutions and reduce their own digital footprint. These efforts will be critical in shaping the role that blockchain plays in building a more sustainable future.

5. TAKING ACTION: HOW YOU CAN ENGAGE WITH ECO-FRIENDLY BLOCKCHAIN SOLUTIONS

5.1: Choosing Green Platforms: Where to Start

As the environmental implications of blockchain become more widely recognized, individuals and organizations are increasingly seeking out **green platforms** that prioritize sustainability. The key to making more eco-conscious choices begins with understanding the types of consensus mechanisms and energy sources that different blockchain networks rely on. Choosing platforms that focus on minimizing their carbon footprint can significantly reduce the environmental impact of engaging with blockchain technology. Below, we will explore how to identify these green platforms and where to start in making more sustainable choices.

The first step in choosing an eco-friendly blockchain platform is to consider networks that use **Proof of Stake (PoS)** rather than **Proof of Work (PoW)**. As we've explored throughout this book, PoS mechanisms are far less energy-intensive because they don't require the enormous computational power used in PoW systems. Popular PoS-based blockchains include **Ethereum (after the Ethereum 2.0 upgrade)**, **Cardano**, and **Tezos**. These networks secure their systems through staked tokens rather than mining, making them a more environmentally responsible choice. **Ethereum's** shift to PoS has dramatically reduced its energy consumption, showcasing how such platforms can scale without the environmental toll.

Beyond consensus mechanisms, it's also important to consider platforms that are actively investing in **carbon offset programs**. For example, **Algorand** is a PoS network that not only operates efficiently but also commits to being carbon-negative by offsetting its emissions through the purchase of carbon credits. Algorand's sustainability pledge makes it one of the greenest blockchains available today, and it demonstrates how platforms can combine technology with environmental responsibility. Similarly, **Chia Network** uses **Proof of Space and Time**, a system that leverages unused hard drive space rather than intensive computational work. This significantly lowers the energy costs associated with securing the network.

It's also worth exploring newer blockchain projects that were built with sustainability in mind from the start. **Celo**, a mobile-first PoS platform, aims to create financial systems accessible to anyone while maintaining a low carbon footprint. Celo's emphasis on eco-consciousness is evident in its dedication to **reforestation projects** and **renewable energy sourcing**, aligning the network's goals with global sustainability efforts. Projects like these are leading the charge in building a blockchain future that doesn't sacrifice environmental responsibility for innovation.

Another key factor in selecting a green platform is transparency regarding energy consumption and sustainability practices. Some blockchain networks publish detailed **sustainability reports**, outlining how they are minimizing their environmental impact. Look for platforms that are open about their energy sources and have clear strategies for reducing their carbon footprint. Networks that incorporate renewable energy sources—such as **Iceland's geothermal energy** for mining or **Canada's hydropower**—demonstrate that sustainability can be integrated into the infrastructure that powers blockchain systems.

Choosing green blockchain platforms is becoming easier as more networks prioritize sustainability. By opting for PoS systems, supporting networks that participate in carbon offset programs, and selecting platforms that prioritize renewable energy, individuals and organizations can significantly reduce their environmental footprint while still benefiting from blockchain's transformative potential. With an increasing number of blockchain projects embracing eco-friendly practices, the future of sustainable blockchain technology is promising.

5.2: Supporting Sustainable Projects: How to Make an Impact

One of the most effective ways to engage with eco-friendly blockchain solutions is by actively supporting projects that focus on **environmental sustainability**. As the blockchain industry grows, several innovative initiatives are emerging that aim to reduce the sector's carbon footprint while also driving positive environmental change. By choosing to back these projects, individuals and organizations can make a tangible impact on the future of blockchain and its relationship with the environment.

One of the most prominent projects in this space is **KlimaDAO**, a decentralized autonomous organization focused on leveraging blockchain to tackle climate change. KlimaDAO uses tokenized **carbon credits** to incentivize individuals and businesses to offset their carbon emissions. Through its native token, **KLIMA**, the platform allows participants to purchase carbon credits on the blockchain, ensuring that these credits are transparently and verifiably retired. KlimaDAO's innovative approach to creating a **carbon-backed cryptocurrency** aligns economic incentives with climate action, making it easier for people to engage with carbon offsetting and contribute to global sustainability efforts.

Another noteworthy project is **Power Ledger**, which utilizes blockchain to facilitate the trade of **renewable energy**. By creating a decentralized energy market, Power Ledger enables individuals and businesses to buy and sell excess solar power directly with one another. This peer-to-peer energy trading model promotes the use of renewable energy sources and reduces reliance on fossil fuels. By supporting platforms like Power Ledger, users are not only engaging with blockchain technology but also contributing to the growth of sustainable energy solutions.

The **Energy Web Foundation (EWF)** is another initiative making strides in the intersection of blockchain and sustainability. EWF focuses on creating decentralized technologies to accelerate the adoption of renewable energy. Their **Energy Web Chain** is a PoS-based blockchain designed specifically for the energy sector, offering tools to manage decentralized energy resources more efficiently. By providing the infrastructure for decentralized energy markets, EWF is helping to create a more sustainable energy grid that aligns with blockchain's core principles of decentralization and transparency.

For those interested in sustainable finance, **Celo** offers another avenue for making an impact. Built as a PoS network, Celo aims to create a more accessible financial system while keeping sustainability at its core. The platform's commitment to environmental responsibility is evident in its participation in **regenerative finance (ReFi)** projects, which focus on combining financial incentives with environmental restoration. Celo has supported several **reforestation projects** and continues to promote the use of blockchain for social and environmental good.

Beyond these well-known projects, there are numerous smaller initiatives making waves in the blockchain sustainability space. For instance, platforms like **Veridium** are working to create blockchain-based marketplaces for carbon credits and other environmental assets. By tokenizing these assets, Veridium aims to increase transparency and accessibility, allowing more people to participate in environmental markets.

Supporting sustainable blockchain projects is a powerful way to contribute to the green movement within the industry. Whether it's through participating in carbon offset programs, trading renewable energy, or backing projects that prioritize environmental restoration, individuals and organizations have a growing number of opportunities to align their blockchain activities with sustainability goals. These projects are not only pushing the boundaries of what blockchain can achieve but are also setting a precedent for how technology can be used as a force for environmental good.

5.3: Reducing Your Digital Footprint: Small Steps for Big Change

While blockchain technology continues to evolve and green platforms are emerging, there are still practical steps individuals can take to minimize their **digital footprint** when engaging with blockchain. Reducing the environmental impact of your blockchain interactions doesn't require large-scale changes—small, intentional actions can make a significant difference. From choosing more sustainable platforms to being mindful of transaction frequency, there are various ways to actively engage in a greener blockchain ecosystem.

One of the most effective ways to reduce your digital footprint is by **limiting the frequency** of transactions. Each blockchain transaction requires energy, especially on **Proof of Work (PoW)** networks like Bitcoin. By consolidating transactions—whether you're sending cryptocurrency or interacting with decentralized applications (dApps)—you can reduce the overall energy required. For example, instead of making multiple small transactions, consider bundling them into one, lowering the demand on the network and, subsequently, the energy needed to validate them.

Another way to reduce your footprint is by being mindful of the type of blockchain platform you use. As discussed earlier, **Proof of Stake (PoS)** networks like **Ethereum**, **Tezos**, and **Cardano** are far less energy-intensive than PoW platforms. If your primary interaction with blockchain involves cryptocurrency transactions or decentralized finance (DeFi) activities, using PoS-based networks can significantly lower your personal contribution to blockchain's energy consumption. Many PoS networks are also transparent about their environmental commitments, making it easier to support platforms that align with your sustainability values.

Using wallets or services that support **Layer 2 solutions** can also help minimize your energy usage. **Layer 2 technologies**, such as the **Lightning Network** for Bitcoin or **Optimistic Rollups** for Ethereum, process transactions off-chain and settle them on the main chain in batches, drastically reducing the energy consumption of each individual transaction. By leveraging these solutions, you can continue to participate in blockchain ecosystems while ensuring that your activities have a reduced environmental impact.

For those involved in mining or staking, consider **choosing renewable energy sources** to power your activities. Some mining operations have already begun relocating to regions where renewable energy is abundant, such as **Iceland** for geothermal power or **Canada** for hydropower. If you are mining on a smaller scale or engaging in staking activities that still require electricity, you can opt to use renewable energy in your home, such as solar panels or wind energy, to offset the energy your devices consume.

Beyond blockchain-specific actions, reducing your overall digital consumption can also have an impact. The energy required to store, manage, and transfer data across the internet, whether for blockchain or other digital services, contributes to global energy consumption. By minimizing your digital footprint across the board—through actions like reducing cloud storage use, turning off devices when not in use, or managing internet-connected devices efficiently—you can contribute to a broader reduction in energy demand.

Another step is supporting platforms and initiatives that focus on **carbon offsets**. Some blockchain projects, such as **Algorand** and **Chia**, are working toward becoming carbon-negative by offsetting their emissions through reforestation projects and other environmental initiatives. By participating in or investing in these platforms, you can ensure that your blockchain activities contribute to projects aimed at mitigating the environmental impact of the technology.

As the blockchain ecosystem continues to mature, individuals have more control than ever over how they engage with the technology. By consolidating transactions, using energy-efficient platforms, leveraging Layer 2 solutions, and supporting renewable energy, you can take small but meaningful steps to reduce your digital footprint. These actions not only help the environment but also encourage the blockchain industry to continue prioritizing sustainability as it grows.

5.4: A Call to Action: Engaging the Blockchain Community for a Greener Future

As blockchain technology continues to evolve, the responsibility to ensure its growth aligns with environmental sustainability doesn't just fall on developers and corporations—**the entire community** can play a role in driving the industry toward a greener future. This final section encourages individuals, organizations, and even policymakers to become active participants in shaping the future of blockchain. By advocating for eco-friendly practices, supporting green initiatives, and holding the industry accountable, we can help steer blockchain in a direction that prioritizes both innovation and environmental responsibility.

One of the most impactful ways to get involved is by **advocating for sustainable practices** within the blockchain communities you're part of. Whether you're a developer, investor, or enthusiast, speaking up about the importance of sustainability can influence decisions made at both the project and network levels. Developers, for example, have the opportunity to integrate energy-efficient protocols like **Proof of Stake (PoS)**, while investors can prioritize funding projects that commit to reducing their carbon footprint. Encouraging discussions around these issues, sharing resources, and pushing for transparency in how projects source their energy are all crucial steps in building a culture of sustainability within the blockchain space.

Another essential avenue for involvement is **supporting regulatory efforts** that aim to make blockchain more sustainable. Governments and policymakers are increasingly aware of blockchain's environmental impact, and there is growing momentum behind proposals to regulate the industry in ways that promote energy efficiency. By backing **carbon taxation policies**, supporting **green blockchain standards**, or advocating for renewable energy incentives for miners, the community can help shape regulations that hold the industry accountable. Engaging in public discourse, submitting comments during regulatory review periods, or even participating in blockchain-focused environmental organizations can have a significant influence on the direction of blockchain policy.

For those looking to make a more immediate impact, **supporting or investing in sustainable blockchain projects** is a tangible way to contribute to a greener future. Projects like **KlimaDAO**, which directly ties blockchain activity to carbon offsetting, or **Energy Web**, which focuses on decentralized energy solutions, are perfect examples of how blockchain can be a force for good in environmental initiatives. By backing these types of projects, you can ensure that your participation in the blockchain space is aligned with efforts to mitigate the technology's environmental impact.

Finally, educating others within and outside of the blockchain space about the importance of sustainability is a key part of driving change. As blockchain adoption grows, so does the need for awareness about its environmental challenges and the solutions that exist. By sharing knowledge, participating in discussions, and promoting eco-conscious blockchain practices, you can help broaden the community's understanding of how blockchain and sustainability can go hand in hand.

The blockchain community is at a crossroads, with the opportunity to choose a future where technological innovation does not come at the expense of the environment. By actively engaging in these efforts and encouraging others to do the same, the community can ensure that blockchain becomes a driving force for positive environmental change. The choices made today will shape the industry's impact for years to come, making it more important than ever for all of us to take action and advocate for a greener, more sustainable blockchain ecosystem.

The community stands at a pivotal moment where it can make meaningful strides toward environmental sustainability. By advocating for greener platforms, supporting sustainable projects, reducing individual digital footprints, and actively promoting regulatory and policy changes, participants in the blockchain space can drive the industry toward a more responsible future. The steps outlined in this chapter highlight how individuals and organizations can become part of this movement, ensuring that blockchain technology evolves without compromising the planet's well-being.

In the final chapter, we will summarize the key takeaways and provide a final reflection on how blockchain's future can balance technological advancement with environmental sustainability. We'll also discuss what lies ahead for blockchain's role in addressing global challenges and the steps that still need to be taken to fully realize its potential as a force for good.

CONCLUSION: BLOCKCHAIN'S GREEN FUTURE—WHAT'S NEXT?

Key Takeaways: Reflecting on Blockchain's Environmental Impact

Throughout this book, we've explored the intricate relationship between blockchain technology and the environment, revealing both the challenges and the solutions that are shaping its future. One of the most critical insights is the sheer **energy consumption** associated with **Proof of Work (PoW)** consensus mechanisms, particularly in networks like Bitcoin. These systems have contributed significantly to blockchain's **carbon footprint**, drawing global attention to the need for change. At the heart of this problem lies the energy-intensive nature of mining, which relies on vast computational power to secure decentralized networks.

However, the rise of **Proof of Stake (PoS)** and other energy-efficient alternatives demonstrates that blockchain's future doesn't have to be at odds with environmental sustainability. Platforms such as **Ethereum**, **Cardano**, and **Tezos** have shown how PoS can drastically reduce energy consumption while maintaining security and decentralization. By shifting away from PoW, these networks are setting a new standard for sustainability in the blockchain space.

Beyond consensus mechanisms, we also examined the role of **green initiatives**, like **carbon offset programs** and the use of **renewable energy** in blockchain mining. Projects like **KlimaDAO** and **Power Ledger** are actively working to offset blockchain's carbon footprint by leveraging decentralized systems to promote environmental sustainability. These efforts highlight how blockchain can be used not only to minimize its own impact but also to support broader climate initiatives.

Another key theme throughout this book is the growing importance of **government regulation** and **policy frameworks**. As blockchain technology continues to expand, it is becoming clear that regulation will play a pivotal role in ensuring that the industry remains environmentally responsible. From **carbon taxation** to **green blockchain standards**, regulatory efforts are essential for holding the industry accountable while encouraging innovation.

Ultimately, the critical takeaway is that blockchain's environmental challenges are not insurmountable. With the right combination of **technological innovation, regulatory oversight,** and **community engagement**, blockchain has the potential to evolve into a powerful tool for both **decentralization** and **sustainability**.

The Road Ahead: What the Future Holds for Blockchain and Sustainability

As blockchain technology continues to advance, the path toward sustainability is becoming clearer. The future of blockchain's environmental impact hinges on **innovative technologies** and the broader adoption of green solutions already taking shape. While the transition from **Proof of Work (PoW)** to more energy-efficient consensus mechanisms like **Proof of Stake (PoS)** has been pivotal, the next wave of technological advancements promises even greater improvements in energy consumption and environmental responsibility.

Emerging technologies such as **zero-knowledge proofs (ZKPs)**, **sharding**, and **Layer 2 scaling solutions** are at the forefront of making blockchain more sustainable. ZKPs, for instance, reduce the amount of data required to validate transactions, decreasing the computational workload and energy required to maintain blockchain networks. Similarly, **Layer 2 solutions** like **Lightning Network** and **Optimistic Rollups** enable transactions to occur off-chain, dramatically reducing the number of transactions that need to be recorded on the main blockchain. These advancements will continue to scale, making blockchain transactions more efficient and eco-friendly.

Looking forward, blockchain's integration with **renewable energy** will play a crucial role in reducing the industry's reliance on fossil fuels. We are already seeing initiatives where blockchain miners are increasingly using **hydropower**, **solar**, and **geothermal** energy sources to power their operations. This trend is likely to accelerate as miners seek both cost savings and reduced environmental impact. Additionally, projects such as **Energy Web** are working to decentralize energy markets, allowing blockchain technology to be part of the solution to global energy challenges.

Another promising area of development is the rise of **regenerative finance (ReFi)**, which seeks to align financial incentives with environmental restoration. Through blockchain-based systems, ReFi projects incentivize investments in climate-positive activities, such as carbon capture, reforestation, and renewable energy. By embedding sustainability into the financial system, ReFi could reshape the blockchain industry, turning it into a key player in fighting climate change.

At the same time, **governments and regulators** will have an increasingly important role in shaping blockchain's environmental future. Policies such as **carbon taxes**, incentives for renewable energy use, and international cooperation on blockchain standards will determine how quickly the industry can transition to greener practices. Collaborative efforts between **governments**, **developers**, and **environmental organizations** will be crucial to ensure that blockchain's growth is aligned with global sustainability goals.

While the challenges ahead are significant, the future holds immense promise for a blockchain industry that can grow in harmony with the environment. With continued investment in green technology, regulatory frameworks, and sustainable development initiatives, blockchain has the potential to become a powerful tool for both innovation and environmental stewardship. The road ahead is one of responsibility, but also one of opportunity for blockchain to contribute to a sustainable future.

The Power of Collective Action: How the Community Can Drive Change

Blockchain's journey toward sustainability cannot be achieved through technology and policy alone. The **community**—from developers to users and advocates—holds significant power in shaping the future of blockchain's environmental impact. Collective action, driven by a shared commitment to sustainability, is essential to ensure that blockchain evolves responsibly. The next steps in the industry's green transformation will depend heavily on the involvement of **individuals, organizations, and the broader blockchain community**.

One of the most critical ways the community can drive change is through **active participation in decision-making processes** within blockchain networks. Many networks, especially decentralized ones like Ethereum, are governed through **decentralized governance** models, where token holders can vote on proposals that shape the network's future. Community members can push for sustainability-focused proposals, such as integrating **carbon offsetting mechanisms** or prioritizing the use of **energy-efficient consensus algorithms**. In networks like **Tezos** or **Polkadot**, where governance is deeply integrated, individuals can make their voices heard and directly influence the direction of the platform's environmental practices.

Beyond governance, the blockchain community can also push for **greater transparency** from the networks and platforms they use. By advocating for clear reporting on **energy consumption, renewable**

energy sourcing, and **carbon offset commitments**, users can help hold blockchain projects accountable for their environmental impact. Supporting platforms that openly share their sustainability metrics and choosing to engage with these eco-conscious networks sends a strong message to the broader industry: environmental responsibility is no longer optional—it's a necessity.

Another key form of collective action is **collaborating with environmental organizations** and supporting blockchain initiatives that focus on sustainability. Many blockchain projects are beginning to partner with environmental nonprofits to further their green agendas. Platforms like **Veridium** and **KlimaDAO** are creating ecosystems that allow individuals to actively participate in **carbon markets**, contributing directly to projects that reduce emissions or promote **reforestation**. By choosing to support these initiatives, blockchain users can help expand the impact of these environmental efforts and incentivize more blockchain companies to follow suit.

Developers and tech enthusiasts also have a unique role to play in shaping the green future of blockchain. By contributing to the development of **energy-efficient protocols** and **Layer 2 scaling solutions**, they can help reduce the environmental footprint of major blockchain networks. The open-source nature of many blockchain projects offers ample opportunity for coders, researchers, and innovators to make a direct contribution to sustainability.

Finally, **education** is key. Spreading awareness about blockchain's environmental challenges and the solutions being developed can inspire more individuals to engage in the movement for sustainability. Whether through hosting events, writing blogs, or sharing resources on social media, community members have the power to raise consciousness about the intersection of blockchain and the environment. A well-informed community can push harder for greener practices, leading to a more sustainable future for the entire industry.

The power of collective action within the blockchain community is immense. By taking active steps to support sustainable practices, individuals can drive the industry forward and ensure that blockchain remains a tool for innovation while also aligning with global environmental goals.

Final Reflections: A Greener, More Sustainable Blockchain Future

As blockchain technology continues to revolutionize industries and reshape how we approach decentralized systems, the environmental challenges it poses are increasingly clear. However, the future of blockchain does not have to be at odds with sustainability. The innovations we've explored throughout this book—**Proof of Stake, Layer 2 solutions, carbon offset initiatives**, and the use of **renewable energy**—demonstrate that it is possible to build blockchain networks that are both powerful and environmentally responsible.

The blockchain industry is at a pivotal moment. With global attention focused on sustainability, blockchain has the opportunity to lead by example and embrace technologies and practices that reduce its carbon footprint. By integrating more energy-efficient systems and promoting transparency in energy use, the blockchain community can align with global efforts to combat climate change while maintaining the integrity and security of decentralized networks.

The next step in blockchain's evolution is not just about **innovating faster or building more applications**—it's about ensuring that the technology is developed with a long-term vision for the planet. This requires collaboration across all levels: developers, miners, regulators, and end-users must all contribute to shaping a future where blockchain can thrive without compromising the environment. By embedding sustainability into the very fabric of blockchain technology, we can create a future where innovation and environmental responsibility go hand in hand.

In the end, blockchain's potential to drive positive change extends far beyond its current applications. From facilitating carbon trading to creating decentralized energy markets, blockchain has the power to be a force for good in the fight against climate change. The key lies in making conscious decisions today—decisions that will shape a greener, more sustainable blockchain ecosystem for future generations.

GLOSSARY OF TERMS

Blockchain: A decentralized, digital ledger that records transactions across multiple computers, ensuring security, transparency, and immutability. Each block of data is linked to the previous one, forming a chain of records.

Carbon Offset Programs: Initiatives where companies or individuals compensate for their carbon emissions by investing in projects that reduce CO_2 elsewhere, such as reforestation or renewable energy initiatives.

Consensus Mechanism: A method used by blockchain networks to agree on the validity of transactions. **Proof of Work (PoW)** and **Proof of Stake (PoS)** are the most common consensus mechanisms.

Decentralized Autonomous Organization (DAO): An organization governed by smart contracts and decisions made collectively by token holders rather than centralized authorities.

Layer 2 Solutions: Technologies built on top of a primary blockchain (Layer 1) that improve scalability and reduce energy consumption by processing transactions off-chain and settling them on-chain later.

Lightning Network: A Layer 2 scaling solution for Bitcoin that allows for faster, cheaper transactions by processing them off-chain and settling only the final transaction on the main Bitcoin blockchain.

Proof of Space and Time (PoST): A consensus mechanism used by networks like Chia, which relies on unused hard drive space (Proof of Space) and the passage of time (Proof of Time) to secure the blockchain, making it more energy-efficient than PoW.

Proof of Stake (PoS): An energy-efficient consensus mechanism where validators are selected based on the amount of cryptocurrency they hold and are willing to "stake" as collateral, reducing the need for computational power.

Proof of Work (PoW): A consensus mechanism used in early blockchains like Bitcoin, where miners solve complex mathematical puzzles to validate transactions and secure the network. PoW is energy-intensive due to the computational power required.

Regenerative Finance (ReFi): A movement within blockchain and finance that aligns financial incentives with environmental restoration, such as funding projects aimed at reducing carbon emissions or restoring ecosystems.

Sharding: A method of partitioning a blockchain into smaller, more manageable pieces (called "shards") to improve scalability and reduce the energy and computational resources required for each transaction.

Zero-Knowledge Proofs (ZKPs): Cryptographic tools that allow one party to prove the truth of a statement to another party without revealing any additional information. ZKPs can help reduce the data processed on-chain, lowering energy consumption.

A FINAL NOTE FROM THE AUTHOR

As we navigate the rapidly evolving world of blockchain technology, one thing is clear: innovation must be balanced with responsibility. Blockchain has already revolutionized industries, offering solutions that were once unimaginable. Yet, like all technological advancements, it comes with challenges—particularly its impact on the environment. The intention behind this book was to explore these challenges head-on and showcase the incredible strides being made to create a more sustainable future for blockchain.

The exciting part about this journey is that we are only at the beginning. There is immense potential for blockchain to contribute to global sustainability goals, from enabling carbon markets to decentralizing renewable energy grids. By investing in greener technologies, advocating for responsible policies, and driving community-led initiatives, we can ensure that blockchain becomes a powerful tool for environmental good.

This book is a call to action—for innovators, investors, users, and policymakers. Together, we can push the boundaries of what blockchain can achieve while ensuring that it aligns with the urgent need to protect our planet. The power of decentralized technology is its ability to empower individuals and communities, and with that power comes a responsibility to act with the future in mind.

Thank you for taking the time to explore this crucial topic with me. I hope this book has provided both insight and inspiration, reminding us all that the choices we make today will shape the technological and environmental landscape of tomorrow.

GET YOUR FREE AUDIOBOOK!

Sign up to an Audible FREE trial using the QR code below and use your first free credit to download a copy of **Crypto's Carbon Conundrum**!

Crypto's Carbon Conundrum on Audible

BOOKS IN THIS SERIES

Explore the exciting and transformative world of cryptocurrencies and decentralized technologies through this comprehensive series.

Each book delves into critical aspects of the blockchain ecosystem, providing insights and knowledge for complete beginners and experienced enthusiasts alike.

Your Crypto Crash Course series on Amazon

1. Your Crypto Crash Course: Fast-Tracking The Journey into Bitcoin, Blockchain, and Beyond

Embark on your cryptocurrency journey with this essential guide designed for newcomers. This book provides a clear and engaging introduction to the foundational concepts of Bitcoin, blockchain technology, and the broader cryptocurrency landscape. Learn the basics of digital currencies, how blockchain works, and the implications of these technologies for the future of finance.

2. Crypto Creations: How Smart Contracts, NFTs, and DeFi Are Shaping the Future

Dive deeper into the innovative applications of blockchain technology with this exploration of smart contracts, non-fungible tokens (NFTs), and decentralized finance (DeFi). Discover how these revolutionary tools are transforming various industries, empowering creators, and reshaping economic systems. This book offers real-world examples and insights into the potential and challenges of these emerging technologies.

3. Web 3.0 Wonders: Your Guide to Unpacking DAOs, Decentralization, and the Metaverse

Uncover the future of the internet with this insightful guide to Web 3.0. Explore the concepts of decentralized autonomous organizations (DAOs), the principles of decentralization, and the metaverse's potential to reshape social interactions and commerce. This book equips readers with the knowledge to understand the technological advancements that promise to redefine how we connect and collaborate in the digital age.

4. Crypto Confidence: A Beginner's Blueprint to Protecting Your Digital Assets

A comprehensive guide covering the fundamental concepts of digital assets, highlights common security threats, and offers practical strategies for safeguarding your investments. With insights into the latest tools, monitoring techniques, and emerging trends, readers will be empowered to protect their digital wealth and confidently engage with the evolving landscape of crypto. Ideal for newcomers and seasoned investors alike, this book is your essential resource for achieving crypto security and success.

5. Crypto's Carbon Conundrum: Blockchain's Battle with the Environment

Examine the environmental impact of blockchain technologies in this thought-provoking book. As the demand for cryptocurrencies and decentralized applications grows, so do concerns about their ecological footprint. This book explores the challenges and solutions for creating sustainable blockchain systems, offering insights into how the industry can address its carbon footprint and contribute to a greener future.

**Your Crypto Crash Course
series on Amazon**

If you find any of these books helpful and enjoyable, please consider leaving a review. Your feedback not only encourages me to write more content for the community but also helps others discover the value of these books. Together, we can foster a knowledgeable and engaged community that navigates the digital currency revolution with confidence.

Thank you for your support, and stay in touch for future free book and preview offers!

GET EXCLUSIVE PREVIEWS!

Download Free Preview Chapters!

As part of the **Your Crypto Crash Course** launch, we're offering **FREE** preview chapters from Books 1-4!

Get Your Exclusive Content!

Don't miss out on this **limited-time offer** to dive into the world of cryptocurrency and blockchain.

ABOUT THE AUTHOR

Ryan J. Carrington is an author from Scotland known for his clear and engaging approach to simplifying complex technological topics. His work demystifies the world of cryptocurrency, blockchain, and digital finance, offering readers practical insights into the future of tech.

With titles spanning introductory crypto guides, explorations of decentralized finance (DeFi), and the environmental impact of blockchain, Ryan combines his expertise in software engineering and passion for accessibility to educate and inspire a broad audience.

His latest works include:
- **Your Crypto Crash Course:** Fast-Tracking The Journey into Bitcoin, Blockchain, and Beyond
- **Crypto Creations:** How Smart Contracts, NFTs, and DeFi Are Shaping the Future
- **Web 3.0 Wonders:** Your Guide to Unpacking DAOs, Decentralization, and the Metaverse
- **Crypto Confidence:** A Beginner's Blueprint to Protecting Your Digital Assets
- **Crypto's Carbon Conundrum:** Blockchain's Battle with the Environment

When he's not writing, Ryan enjoys hiking in the mountains near his home in Inverness, Scotland, reading sci-fi novels, and traveling to experience new cultures.

Made in the USA
Columbia, SC
14 February 2025